CHESTER
CITY GUIDE

Alistair and Jan Campbell

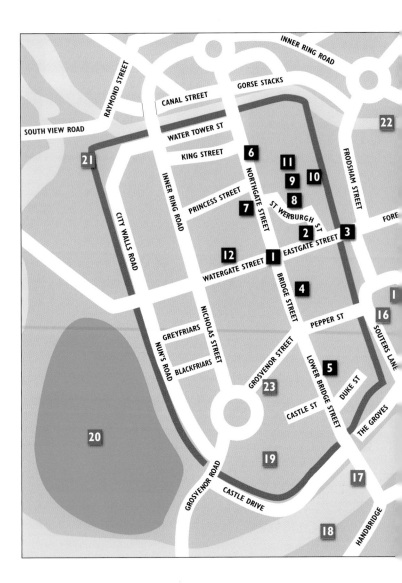

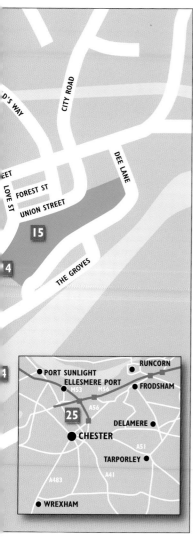

CONTENTS

Tourist Office

Town Hall

Cathedral

MARKET P...

Town Hall

INTRODUCTION

ANTIQUI COLANT ANTIQUUM DIERUM
(Let the Ancients Worship the Ancient of Days)

A stroll around the largest unbroken stretch of city walls in Britain will help unfold some of Chester's history as a former major seaport, military garrison and city under siege. The influence of the city's heritage is very much evident throughout its streets, lanes and architecture, with its principal thoroughfares still bearing a strong resemblance to their original historic design. Its famous and unique two-tiered Rows continue to maintain the city's ancient reputation as a thriving commerce-based community. Neither the canal nor River Dee is now burdened with the responsibility of supporting shipbuilding and manufacturing industries, but their picturesque banks and locks provide an idyllic setting for an array of sporting and leisure activities.

Located within the county of Cheshire and in close proximity to the North Wales border, the city of Chester owes much of its status as a prominent and favoured tourist destination to its long and enthralling history. Deva, one of three Roman legionary fortresses in Britain, was established in the late 70s AD. The strategic military position and importance of the site was to become the foundation of Chester's future heritage, providing an almost 2,000-year chronological diary of life as a Cestrian. The city's autobiography spans the Roman, Saxon, Norman, mediaeval, Tudor, Stuart, Georgian and Victorian eras through to the present day.

City Wall Tour

Chester is often referred to as 'The Walled City', and at just over 3km (approximately 2 miles) in length the city has the most complete circuit of walls in Britain. A gentle stroll around the city walls will reveal a fascinating history that spans from Chester's Roman Fortress origins through to the Saxon and mediaeval periods. More recent Georgian and Victorian cosmetic alterations have transformed the wall from its original protective role to a fashionable and popular promenade, although the ramparts still bear the scars of cannon bombardment and defence breaches. There are lots to see both on and away from the wall, which provides spectacular elevated views of the city streets, Roman amphitheatre, Old Dee Bridge, River Dee, Chester Canal, Roman Gardens and

even magnificent views across to Wales. In recognition of their archaeological importance, Chester city walls have been designated as a Scheduled Ancient Monument.

It is possible to join and leave the wall walk in many locations, and although not an essential starting point, standing on the wall under the Eastgate Clock [1] looking west along Eastgate Street towards the High Cross, will provide the viewer with their first stunning prominent vista of the city. This elevated view of the street's contrasting architecture and bustling pavements is often considered as one of the finest inner-city views in all of England.

Continuing your tour of the walls in a clockwork route from the Eastgate Clock will shortly bring you to Newgate [2].

Built in the late 1930s as part of a city traffic enhancement scheme, the Newgate offers a good view of the Roman amphitheatre, St John the Baptist Church – Chester's first cathedral – and beyond to Grosvenor Park. Adjacent to the Newgate is the 17th-century Wolfgate, the mediaeval Thimbleby's Tower and the remains of a Roman angle tower. Steps at the Newgate will allow exploration of the Roman Gardens, Grosvenor Park, Roman amphitheatre and St John's Church.

Slightly beyond Newgate on your left is the Roman Gardens [3], while on your right are the mid-17th-century almshouses known as the Nine Houses [4], of which there are only six now remaining.

Further along the wall towards the River Dee you will pass the Watch Tower [5], which was subject to fierce attack during the Civil War. Indeed, the base of the tower still bears the scars of cannonball bombardment and musket fire. The Watch Tower affords clear views of the River Dee and the Groves towards Queen's Bridge.

Continuing the tour from the Watch Tower you descend a series of six short flights of steps known as the Wishing Steps [6].

Constructed as part of a promenade project in 1785, the Wishing Steps join two different levels of the wall. Folklore states that if you run up and down the steps without taking a breath, then your wish will come true. This is apparently a particularly popular myth among ladies who are seeking wedlock.

Now walking parallel with the River Dee and slightly further along from the Wishing Steps is another promenade trail enhancement, the Recorder Steps [7]. These were added to the wall in the early 1700s, allowing walkers easy access between the wall and the Groves [8]. Indeed, if desired, this is an ideal location to briefly leave the wall and explore the Groves, River Dee [9], Old Dee Bridge [10] and Edgar's Field.

A little beyond the Recorder Steps is the Round Tower [11]. Once a mediaeval watch tower, the elevated position offers superb views over the Norman weir, River Dee, Old Dee Bridge and beyond towards Edgar's Field.

On route towards Chester Castle, you cross over Bridgegate [12] and continue past the County Hall [13].

Built in 1782, the Bridgegate was designed by Joseph Turner, who was also

responsible for the Watergate. Being the only mediaeval route from the city into North Wales ensured that the Bridgegate's predecessors, also known as the Welshgate and South Gate, were heavily fortified and defended.

The wall route continues past the front of County Hall, but the section of wall at Castle Drive was demolished in 1901 and is considered the only break in the wall circuit. County Hall was built on the site of the former gaol. Although construction of the building began in the 1930s it was not totally completed until 1957.

Immediately after passing County Hall the walls and motte of Chester

Castle [14] will appear on your right-hand side. The principle and very grand entrance to the castle grounds is located on Grosvenor Road.

Crossing at the traffic lights on Grosvenor Road, you continue along the wall tour adjacent to Chester Racecourse (the Roodee) [15] until reaching the Watergate [16].

Built in 1788 by Joseph Turner, who also designed the Bridgegate, the Watergate replaced a mediaeval West Gate. Prior to canalisation the River Dee met the City Walls at this point.

While en route between the Watergate and Bonewaldesthorne's Tower, look out for the Sedan House [17], Queen's School and the former Royal Infirmary, all of which are situated on City Walls Road.

The Sedan House is so named because of its two-door porch which allowed the bearers of a sedan chair to enter the building through one door and stop outside the facing door, thus allowing a passenger to alight inside the building.

Designed by E.A. Ould, the brown brick and red terracotta Queen's School [18] stands on the site of the old city gaol. Queen Victoria ordered its name to be changed from 'The Chester School for Girls' to 'The Queen's School'.

The former Chester Royal Infirmary [19] has now been converted to residential apartments. Royal was added to the infirmary's name after King George V opened a new wing of the hospital in 1914.

Reaching the north-west corner of the walls brings into view Bonewaldesthorne's Tower [20]. The structure was originally located at the banks of the River Dee but silting of the river made it necessary to build another watch tower in 1322. The Water Tower [21] is placed on a spur wall from Bonewaldesthorne's Tower to the then location of the river. As the river further silted and receded the Water Tower was also left stranded. A better view of the Water Tower can be achieved from the Water Tower Gardens [22], which can be reached via nearby steps. Access to Chester Canal basin – part of the Shropshire Union Canal – is also within easy reach of the gardens.

Leaving Bonewaldesthorne's behind, the route now continues along the northern section of the

walls, which run parallel with the canal. The first point of interest on this stretch of the tour is Pemberton's Parlour [23], which is the site of a mediaeval watch tower. The tower is named after the owner of a rope works who would survey his workers as they laboured below. However, Pemberton's Parlour has also previously been named Dille's Tower and Goblin Tower. A carved inscription on the stone states that the tower was rebuilt in 1894.

Shortly after this tower you cross over the top of the busy inner-city road at St Martins Way. St Martins Gate footbridge [24] is a relatively modern addition to the walls and was built in the 1960s to facilitate the construction of a dual carriageway which was deemed essential to deal with an ever-increasing volume of road traffic.

Soon after crossing the footbridge, the next structure of interest is Morgan's Mount [25]. This watch tower is believed to be named after Captain Morgan, a Royalist gun battery commander who defended the city from this position during the Civil War, 1642–46.

The route then moves onwards to the Northgate [26] where you return to city centre views looking south down Northgate Street. Built by Thomas Harrison in 1810, the arched Northgate replaced a former mediaeval gate. Access to street level is available from the bridge and will allow the opportunity to gain further views of the nearby Blue Coal School [27] and Bridge of Sighs [28].

Continuing from Northgate you pass over remnants of the original Roman wall, which is best viewed from the bridge over the canal at Northgate. King Charles Tower [29], at the north-east corner of the wall, is where King Charles I is believed to have stood and witnessed his army being defeated, or pursued, by Parliamentary troops during the battle of Rowton Moor in 1645. The tower was also known as Phoenix Tower after a carved stone phoenix, which was the emblem of Chester's Guild of Painters.

This final leg of the wall walk passes alongside Deanery Fields [30], which are part of the Cathedral precinct and lead to a rear view of Chester Cathedral [31]. Notice how the Cheshire Regiment Garden of Remembrance [32] flower beds are laid out in the shape of a medal. Access to the main cathedral entrance and grounds can be achieved via the steps at the Cathedral bell tower [33].

Continuing the walk a little further to the Eastgate Clock [34] completes your circuit of Chester City Walls. Leaving the wall at Eastgate will allow further exploration of the city streets, shops, Rows, gardens and landmarks, many of which are detailed within this guide.

City Streets

Chester's street pattern still bears a striking resemblance to its original Roman and mediaeval layout. The High Cross is considered the centre of the city where Eastgate, Northgate, Watergate and Bridge Street all converge. Renowned for its black-and-white timber-framed building façades, each of these four arterial streets contributes to a Tudor theme that is prevalent throughout the city. However, there is a definite architectural contrast, with each street having its own history, landmarks, character and tales to tell. The shared trends along each route are undoubtedly retail and leisure. This traditionally commerce-based city centre is strongly supported by Chester's unique two-tier shopping levels known as the Rows. With the exception of Northgate Street, the Rows can be found on both sides of each street.

High Cross

Chester High Cross dates from approximately 1377, although the Parliamentarians deliberately demolished the original cross after the Civil War. Partially restored and retained in the Roman Gardens, the High Cross was finally returned to its City Centre location in 1975. Parts of the original structure have never been recovered.

Eastgate Street

Eastgate Street is a mixture of contrasting architectural building styles and has been compared with some of London's finest shopping streets; indeed, Chester's

High Cross

largest department store, Browns of Chester, is nicknamed the 'Harrods of the North'. The area is partially pedestrianised with restricted vehicle access, allowing the easy ebb and flow of workers and shoppers. There is lots to see as you stroll towards the High Cross, and your short journey is often graced with the sound and sight of talented buskers. All along the street protrudes a number of former tramway brackets that were used to power the electric trams until their replacement by buses in 1930. The ornate brackets are now being used to suspend shop and hotel signs. Keep an eye open for the, Ye Old Boot Inn which was established in 1643 and is one of the oldest surviving public houses in Chester.

Eastgate Clock

Designed by John Douglas, the Eastgate Clock is arguably Chester's most famous landmark. Erected in 1899 to commemorate Queen Victoria's 1897 Diamond Jubilee, the aesthetic open wrought-iron structure makes it difficult to resist the temptation of a quick photograph, helping to confirm its reputation as the most photographed clock, after Big Ben, in the world.

Bridge Street

Leading from the High Cross to the Bridgegate at the Old Dee Bridge, via Lower Bridge Street, Bridge Street resumes the retail theme synonymous with the other principal streets. The galleried walkways of the Bridge Street Rows extend the whole length on both sides of the street, each connecting with their neighbouring galleried rows

on south Eastgate and south Watergate. The entire length of the street down to the Bridgegate is worthy of viewing.

Starting from the High Cross, the black-and-white timbered Tudor-style reconstructed buildings at No.1 Bridge Street are believed to be the most photographed scene, after the Eastgate Clock, in Chester.

A 13th-century crypt at No.12 Bridge Street is thought to be one of the oldest in the city and is also rumoured to be haunted. The crypt has been utilised for many retail purposes including a bookstore, luxury accessories boutique and ladies' fashion store.

Grosvenor Shopping Centre's Bridge Street entrance leads to St Michaels Row. Built for the second Duke of Westminster in 1910, the Grosvenor Shopping Centre's original tiled façade met with fierce public disapproval, eventually leading to the tiles being replaced with the current timber-framed frontage. However, the tiles on the elegant Edwardian arcade of St Michaels Row were retained.

Originally a mediaeval town house, the 'Three Old Arches' at pavement and row levels are believed to be the oldest surviving shop façade in England. The arches are dated AD1274.

The 13th-century crypt

Grosvenor Shopping centre

St Michaels Row

Lifting your eyes above street level on the opposite side of the street to the Three Old Arches, you should spot a carving of King Charles I. When the carpenters came to install the carving, they found that it was too tall for its recess and had to shorten the legs to make it fit.

Tudor House

Lower Bridge Street

Lower Bridge Street Rows have all but disappeared. A combination of cafés, bars and restaurants are interspersed with specialist retail outlets. The street contains a number of buildings and structures of architectural and historical interest. Starting at the corner near the traffic lights is the Falcon Inn, which was almost entirely derelict before being rescued and restored. The inn was reopened by the Duke of Westminster in 1992. During its long history the structure has been utilised for many purposes and is recorded as being the first building to have its Rows enclosed to prevent public access.

Park House

Slightly further down on the opposite side of the street is Tudor House, a timber-framed town house which was constructed in the early 1600s for a wealthy merchant. A plaque on the wall dating the build as 1503 is supposedly incorrect.

Ye old Kings Head

Easily identifiable by its Tuscan porch, Park House is an early 18th-century Georgian town house. Its history of use includes a private residence, hotel, ladies' academy, antiques emporium, wine bar and offices. The Duke of Wellington reputedly stayed in the building when it was being used as the Albion Hotel in 1820.

At the lower end of the street there are a few public houses of notable interest including Ye Old Kings Head, which is much older than its first licence to sell alcohol in 1717 indicates.

Another public house and restaurant is the Bear and Billet, which was originally the Earl of Shrewsbury's residence. Named after the Earl's heraldic device of a shackled bear, this mid-17th-century building has a Dutch architectural influence.

Northgate Street

Northgate Street leads from the centre of the city to the Northgate and Fountains Roundabout. In addition to the many retail outlets, cafes, restaurants and pubs, the street offers access to the Forum Shopping Centre, Town Hall and Chester Cathedral.

Northgate Street contains the shortest surviving stretch of Rows in all four galleried row streets. The rows on the west side, near Eastgate Street, were demolished, partially to make way for the Commercial Newsroom.

Originally opening in 1808 as a subscription library, news and coffee room, the Greek

Commercial Newsroom

Revival-style frontage of the Commercial Newsroom was designed by Thomas Harrison, the same architect responsible for the redesign of the Chester Castle complex. The adjoining black-and-white-fronted Shoemakers Row was rebuilt at the turn of the 20th century and is named after the predominate product being produced and traded by its craftsmen.

A favoured meeting place and lunchtime haunt is the Market Square, which holds periodic continental and local markets and offers splendid vistas of both the Chester Cathedral and the Town Hall. The square is also dominated by the Stephen Broadbent sculpture *A Celebration of Chester*. The three carved figures represent 'Thanksgiving, Protection and Industry', with protection facing the Town Hall. Thanksgiving is placed centrally between the other two figures and facing towards the cathedral – this is said to represent the 'spiritual life of the individual and the group'. The Industry figure reaches downwards to the ground, representing the 'work and effort of every citizen'.

Town Hall

Adjacent to the Forum Shopping Centre is Chester Town Hall, designed by the Belfast architect W.H. Lynn. The Town Hall was opened in 1869 by the Prince of Wales with the Prime Minister of that time, W.E. Gladstone, in attendance. The impressive façade of this Victorian Gothic-style building has an equally striking interior. The Tourist Information Centre is located at the south end of the Town Hall.

Near the city library stands a Roman column and bases which commemorate a European award to Chester for the 'preservation of historic monuments'.

Library and Roman Column

Town Hall

Chester Library

The attractive brick and terracotta façade of the former Westminster Coach and Motor Car Works is now the home of Chester Library.

Built circa early 17th century and billed as a traditional coaching inn, the Pied Bull Hotel is believed to be Chester's oldest surviving public house, there are also rumours that it is haunted. Almost adjacent to the hotel is the Blue Bell building, which dates from the late 15th century.

Slightly beyond the Northgate are the Bridge of Sighs and Blue Coat School.

This stone footbridge high above the canal was known as the Bridge of

Pied Bull Hotel

Bridge of Sighs

Sighs and connected the gaol to the chapel of St John in the Blue Coat School.

Constructed on a demolished hospital site, the Blue Coat School was Chester's oldest purpose-built school. Founded by Bishop Stratford as a charity school for poor boys in 1700, the school is still being used as an educational facility by Chester University.

Blue Coat School

St Werburgh Street

Home of Chester Cathedral, St Werburgh Street is named after a Mercian princess who became a nun and later an Abbess. The street leads from Northgate Street back to Eastgate Street and contains a variety of shops and restaurants. Godstall Lane, an attractive narrow lane leading from St Werburgh back to Eastgate Rows, also supports a variety of cafés, restaurants and shops, where it is possible to dine alfresco with the cathedral as a backdrop.

Chester Cathedral

From Saxon Minster to the Benedictine Abbey of Saint Werburgh, worship has taken place on the site of Chester Cathedral for over 1,000 years. The cathedral was transformed from the Benedictine Abbey of St Werburgh to the foundation of Chester Cathedral by Henry VIII during the Dissolution in 1541. The building and site has undergone many transformations but is said to 'contain materials from every Christian century since the tenth'. Major restoration during the late 1800s and again in 1900s has changed the appearance of the cathedral and also caused some architectural controversy. Chester

Cathedral is officially known as the Cathedral of Christ and the Blessed Virgin Mary. Located at the junction of Northgate Street and St Werburgh Street, this magnificent tourist attraction and important place of worship has been open to tourists for almost a hundred years.

Internal viewing of the cathedral will reveal many original Norman and late mediaeval features. There is a magnificent combination of new and old stained-glass windows. Look closely and you will also see the Chester Imp carved into the stone near one of the nave windows – the figure is said to frighten the Devil away. There is a fascinating collection of mediaeval oak carvings in the Quire. One example of a wooden elephant was obviously carved by a craftsman who had never seen the real animal, believing that an elephant had the legs and hooves of a horse.

Addleshaw Bell Tower

Addleshaw Bell Tower

Designed by George Pace, the Chester Cathedral Addleshaw Bell Tower was named after a Cathedral Dean. The tower was built in 1975 after it was discovered that the cathedral's own tower was no longer able to support the bells. Located in the Cathedral Gardens, it is said to be the first bell tower to be built separately from an English cathedral since the 1600s.

Abbey Square

The 14th-century Abbey Gateway leads from Northgate Street to Abbey Square. This was the former site of the

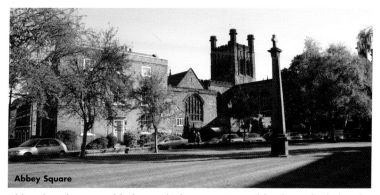

Abbey Square

Abbey brewhouse and bakery, which was converted by the cathedral in the 18th century to a square of smart residential properties – now mostly offices. The cobbled street is lined with York stone, known as wheelers, which were designed to assist the transit of horse and carriage.

Watergate Street

Watergate Street leads from the High Cross to the Watergate and Chester Racecourse, via New Crane Street. Outlets along the street and Rows are very diverse with goods and services ranging from vintners, silverware, antiques, art galleries, jewellers and furniture to excellent public houses, restaurants, cafés and bistros. Watergate Street has some magnificent architectural buildings.

Starting from the High Cross towards the Watergate, you will find God's Providence House on the south side of the street. Originally built in 1652 the structure was rebuilt much later with the intention of retaining some semblance of its original façade. The house name and external inscription 'God's Providence is Mine Inheritance'

God's Providence House

View from
Watergate St
Rows towards
the High Cross

is said to have originated from a family who survived the plague.

Leche House, a mediaeval town house, dates from the late 14th century.

The timber-framed Bishop Lloyd's Palace was built for George Lloyd, Bishop of Chester and also Bishop of Sodor and Man (an historic diocese of the Church of England). Originally completed in approximately 1615, the structure was subjected to major refurbishment in 1899. It is now the headquarters of Chester Civic Trust, who encourage public viewing of the building interior at specified times.

Leche House

Located in the former Holy Trinity Church is the Guildhall. Chester's historic guilds have over 800 years of history and economic influence. Non-guild craftsmen or traders were not permitted to work or sell their goods in Chester without paying a levy or attending the summer and autumn fairs. Guild members have revived the ancient tradition of performing the Chester Mystery Plays – previously banned in the 1570s – which are performed every five years. The Guildhall houses a small but interesting museum, which offers free entry to the general public on request.

Bishop Lloyd's Palace

At the bottom of Watergate Street is Ye Old Custom House Inn, which dates from 1637. The inn changed its name in the 18th century to reflect its position opposite the Port of Chester custom house.

Guildhall

Landmarks

Roman Amphitheatre

Accidentally unearthed during building works in 1929, Britain's largest partially excavated amphitheatre is now a major city centre landmark and tourist attraction. Utilised to entertain and train the Roman military, an original wooden structure with seating for 2,000 people was later replaced, around AD 100, with a stone amphitheatre enabling a much larger audience capacity of approximately 7,000. Excavation of the site has periodically been undertaken since the amphitheatre's discovery. A project to learn more about the amphitheatre, and its neighbouring Grosvenor Park, is planned to continue for the foreseeable future.

St John's

One of the oldest religious sites in Chester, this former Saxon Minster, now the Church of St John the Baptist, is believed to date from the 7th century, making it one of Chester's oldest surviving structures. St John's became Chester's first cathedral in 1075, but only remained so until 1102. Evidence suggests that the original structure of the church was constructed with building

materials taken from the nearby Roman amphitheatre. Restoration work in the 19th century gives this Norman church a Victorian appearance. Ruins at both sides of St John's are from previous tower collapses dating from the 14th, 15th and 19th centuries.

This magnificent structure is best appreciated from inside the church, where much of its Norman heritage is still evident.

Among St John's more modern acquisitions is one of the organs used for Queen Victoria's Coronation at Westminster Abbey in 1838. The organ was purchased after the great event and transported to its current location.

Grosvenor Park

Grosvenor Park is a 19th-century Victorian-designed 20-acre public recreational area. Opened in 1867, the park was originally gifted to the city by Richard Grosvenor, the Second Marquis of Westminster.

The park contains ancient arches that have been relocated from their original sites, including the former west door of St Michael's Church,

Grosvenor Park Lodge is located at the Grosvenor Park Road and Union Street junction entrance to the park.

Originally known as the Park Keeper's Lodge, this black and white half-timbered building was designed by John Douglas, who also designed the Eastgate Clock. The building is decorated with wood carvings of William the Conqueror and the Norman Earls of Chester.

Roman Gardens

Constructed in 1949 adjacent to the City Wall, the Roman Gardens were created to display an array of Roman columns and bases that had been discovered throughout the city. This secluded location proves to be a popular tourist attraction and lunchtime haunt for city workers. In addition to the various Roman columns and bases there is also a reconstructed hypocaust (under-floor heating system). Many of the plants, shrubs and trees contained within the formal garden have a Roman theme or association.

Old Dee Bridge

Old Dee Bridge

Built c.1387, the Old Dee Bridge is a Grade 1 Listed Scheduled Ancient Monument and an important mediaeval city landmark. Extending from Bridgegate to Handbridge, the bridge still retains its tollgate post were tolls continued to be charged for crossing until 1885.

Edgar's Field

Named after King Edgar who ascended to the throne in 959, Edgar's Field was donated to Chester as a public park by the 1st Duke of Westminster in 1892. The park contains a Roman shrine to the goddess Minerva. Adjacent to the River Dee, this 2 ¼ acre recreational area affords excellent views over the river towards the Old Dee Bridge and the city.

Chester Castle

Agricola Tower

Originally built by the Normans in approximately 1070, the castle underwent major reconstruction from 1780. Thomas Harrison, the architect responsible for the redesign, replaced the dilapidated mediaeval gaol and Shire Hall, previously known as the Great Hall, with a much admired group of Greek Revival buildings fronted by an impressive propylaeum-style gateway.

The building project began in a piecemeal fashion in 1788 but was not fully completed until 1822. Some semblance of the castle's mediaeval history is still evident within Chester Castle's

Chester Castle
gateway

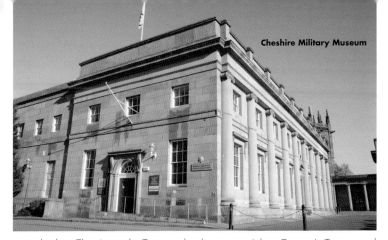

inner bailey. The Agricola Tower, also known as Julius Caesar's Tower and Julius Agricola's Tower, stands at the entrance to the inner bailey.

Chester Castle's Harrison Block is home to the Cheshire Military Museum. The museum contains exhibitions relating to the Cheshire Regiment, Cheshire Yeomanry, 5th Royal Inniskilling Dragoon Guards, 3rd Carabiniers, Eaton Hall Officer Cadet School and other smaller military Cheshire units.

Chester Racecourse

Dating from the 16th century, Chester Racecourse on the Roodee is reputed to be the oldest racecourse in England. Its circular layout ensures that race-goers have the unique visual advantage of being able to see the whole course without the aid of binoculars – the oval-shaped course also earned it the nickname of 'Soup-Plate'. Situated on the former Roman port, the course aptly illustrates how the river has changed course over the centuries.

49

Water Tower Garden

Built on reclaimed land during the Victorian period, Water Tower Gardens is a designated conservation area, which also contains a Roman-influenced dolphin mosaic at the centre of a coloured maze.

Chester Canal

Continual silting of the River Dee, combined with the development of the Port of Liverpool and other major canal construction projects, began to undermine Chester's position as a major sea port. This threat to the city's sea trade partially provided the impetus to build a canal link from Chester to Nantwich.

Work began on the canal in 1772 but the whole project was fraught with financial, engineering and planning problems. Although not the originally planned route, a 16-mile Chester to Nantwich canal was finally completed in 1779; however, the project was considered an economic failure. It was not until the expansion of a link between Chester and Ellesmere Port, which now forms part of the Shropshire Union Canal, in the late 18th century, that the canal established itself as successful commercial venture. The Ellesmere Port link became an extremely popular and profitable passenger and cargo route. The arrival of a railway link to Chester in 1840 created competition for the canal and eventually led to its commercial demise. However, there have been new initiatives to regenerate the canal routes for leisure and sporting activities, both on the canal's water and its towpath.

Chester Town Crier

The tradition of reading Noon Proclamations from Chester High Cross dates from the 16th century. Although the ritual ceased in the late 19th century, the position of Chester Town Crier was re-established in 1978. Noon Proclamations take place at the High Cross from Tuesdays to Saturdays between May and August.

Grosvenor Museum

Named after the 1st Duke of Westminster, Lupus Grosvenor, the Grosvenor Museum was built in 1885–86. Dominated by an impressive life-size Roman Centurion in an aggressive stance, the entrance hallway leads to a variety of ground and upper level display exhibitions and galleries. 'A House Through Time' exhibition within the Period House area of the museum aptly illustrates life in a gentry townhouse during different eras.

Exhibited in the Webster Roman Stones Gallery, the museum is especially renowned for 'the largest collection of Roman tombstones from a single site'. Before been recovered and displayed at the museum, virtually all of the tombstones had been utilised to repair the City Wall.

River Dee

The River Dee's 70-mile journey from source to sea begins in North Wales. Its relatively short but impressive passage through Chester is via the Meadows, under the Queen's Park Suspension Bridge, flowing parallel to the Groves, surging over the Norman Weir, passing through the Old Dee Bridge, sweeping far beneath the Grosvenor Bridge, meandering around Chester Racecourse before finally returning back into North Wales. The dramatic influence that the river has contributed to the city's history and fortune is not instantly obvious; however, the route is at the very least scenic and at times absolutely stunning.

A two-mile long pedestrianised promenade trail running parallel to the river begins, or ends, at the Grosvenor Rowing Club. The Groves section of the promenade is home to an abundance of small cafés and restaurants, which offer a selection of fine food, refreshments and excellent views of the river's many waterborne activities. There is ample opportunity for nautical adventures with River Dee cruise trips, paddle, rowing and motorboat hire. The Queen's Park Suspension Bridge was completed in 1923 and is the only footbridge over Chester's span of the Dee. The bridge has become a familiar landmark of the city and has been the backdrop for many television productions.

Cattle graze freely upon the unique, city-centre-located 24 hectare public recreation area known as 'The Meadows'. Due to the nature of the land and habitat it has been designated as a Site of Biological Importance.

Constructed around 1092, the Norman weir provided a head of water to power grinding wheels at nearby flour mills. Located alongside the weir is a section of the migration route for Atlantic salmon known as the Salmon Steps or Salmon Leap.

Constructed in the early 20th century, the steps help the fish to negotiate the weir and reach their spawning ground in the headwaters of the River Dee.

Opened by Princess Victoria in 1832, Grosvenor Bridge was at one time the widest single span bridge in Europe. The designer, Thomas Harrison, died before the bridge was completed.

It is shortly after its meander around the racecourse that the river continues its course along a 200-year-old man-made diversion, known as the 'New Cut', to North Wales and its short journey into Liverpool Bay.

Norman Weir

Grosvenor Bridge

Queen's Bridge and the River Dee

Chester Zoo

There are over 7,000 animals and 500 species at Chester Zoo's 110 acre zoological gardens. Located three miles from the city centre, Britain's largest

garden zoo is an award-winning and extremely popular visitor attraction that is renowned for its conservation outreach programmes.

CHESTER City Beautiful

Explore more of Chester with *Chester City Beautiful*. This impressive publication is packed with a host of information relating to many of Chester's historical landmarks. With a foreword by His Grace the Duke of Westminster, *Chester City Beautiful* contains over 300 high quality artistically pleasing photographs and is considered the definitive pictorial guide to the city.

Each page of *Chester City Beautiful* colourfully and aesthetically portrays a scene, personality, landmark or tradition associated with this unique city.

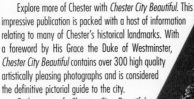

Available at all good bookshops.

First published in Great Britain in 2010 by The Derby Books Publishing Company Limited, 3 The Parker Centre, Mansfield Road, Derby, DE21 4SZ.

© Alistair and Jan Campbell, 2010

All Rights Reserved. No part of this publication may be reproduced, stored in a retrieval system, or transmitted in any form, or by any means, electronic, mechanical, photocopying, recording or otherwise without the prior permission in writing of the copyright holders, nor be otherwise circulated in any form or binding or cover other than in which it is published and without a similar condition being imposed on the subsequent publisher.

A catalogue record for this book is available from the British Library.

ISBN 978-1-85983-849-5

Printed and bound by DZS Grafik, Slovenia.